THE MONKEY KING

f

f

Children and adults alike, we all love stories. When we share a story with children we can help them to explore important areas of human experience and encourage them in their spiritual and moral development. The Greek myths, stories from the Bible, and the countless tales of the world's many religions show that humanity has long used story to communicate its deepest values and codes of behaviour. The magical qualities of a story speak directly to our hearts and illustrate and share profound truths. Imaginatively entering another's world, we return with insights to apply to our own lives.

We have enjoyed writing and illustrating this story from the Buddhist tradition. We hope you and your children will enjoy it too.

Adiccabandhu & Padmasri

Published in association with
The Clear Vision Trust
by Windhorse Publications
11 Park Road
Birmingham B13 8AB

Text and illustrations
© Clear Vision Trust 1998
Design Dhammarati
Illustrations Adiccabandhu
Printed by Interprint Ltd,
Marsa, Malta

British Library Cataloguing in
Publication Data. A catalogue
record for this book is available
from the British Library
ISBN 1 899579 09 5

THE MONKEY KING

Adiccabandhu & Padmasri

WINDHORSE PUBLICATIONS

Far away in the East there once lived a band of monkeys. One day some of the little monkeys were playing in the forest when suddenly the smallest of them spotted a fruit tree. Its branches were full of beautiful golden fruit. It was a mango tree.

"Look, sister!" called the little monkey, "What luck! Just as I was getting hungry, too."

"Stop!" said his big sister. "Don't eat it. The fruit might be bad for you. Let's take one back to our king. He'll know if it's good to eat."

Off ran the young monkeys to find the monkey king.

"Hello, my little ones," said the monkey king. "Back so soon from your playing?"

"Look, look," gasped the smallest one. "I've found this delicious looking fruit."

"... and we've brought it to show to you," said his big sister.

"Is it safe to eat?" she asked.

"Well done," said the monkey king. "How clever of you both." He took the beautiful golden mango in his hand and inspected it carefully.

"What smooth skin it has!" he observed.

He sniffed it. "It smells lovely too. I'll taste it to see if it's safe to eat!"

He took a bite of the golden mango.

"Umm-HMMHH!... Lovely! Here, you have a taste. Are there any more like this?" he asked.

"Oh yes, hundreds of them." said the little one. "Let's go!"

And the monkey band set off into the forest.

They soon found their way back to the
tree. Its long branches spreading out over
the river.

"What a beautiful tree!" said the monkey
king. "Why don't we all live here?"

At once, the monkeys climbed up into the
branches. They all wanted to taste the
beautiful golden fruit.

"Be careful," called the monkey king.
"Don't let any fruit drop into the water."

"But there's lots of fruit," replied the little
one.

"Yes, but what if one of these lovely fruits
fell into the river? It would float away to
where the humans live. Someone might
taste it and come looking for this tree. Let
us first pick all the fruit that hangs over the
river. Then we will be safe."

All that summer, the monkey band lived happily in the mango tree. They played in its shade by day. They slept in its branches by night. Everyone took care not to drop any fruit into the water.

But, hidden behind a leaf, one last mango was still hanging over the river. No one had seen it. One night, when everyone was fast asleep, a breeze shook the branches of the tree.
Plop! Down fell the mango into the water. The golden mango bobbed along in the moonlight carried swiftly and silently downstream.

A few days later the king of the humans was bathing in the river when one of his servants spotted the mango floating by. "Look, your majesty," he called, "something golden in the water!"

The king picked up the mango.
"What's this?" he demanded. "A very strange looking fruit."
He sniffed it.
"It smells good. I wonder if it's safe to eat?"
He turned to his servant.
"Here, taste that!" he commanded.
The guard took a bite.
"Well?"
"Very good, your majesty."

"Now give back it to me!" snapped the king.
No sooner had the king tasted the fruit than he wanted more.
"I want to find that fruit tree," he shouted greedily, "and I want it NOW! The tree must be somewhere up river. We will make a raft and find it. Begin at once!"

Up river, in the mountain forest, the monkeys rested peacefully
in the mango tree. Suddenly, one of the little ones playing in the
branches above saw something.
"Come quickly, come quickly," he called.
From the top of the tree he could see the rafts coming up the
river.

"Quiet everybody," said the monkey king. "The humans are coming. They've got bows and arrows. We will have to hide high up in the branches until they have gone."

All day long the king's men picked the fruit. The monkeys hid in the leaves above.

At last, the king stood up.

"It's been a long day," he yawned, "Make a bed for me under the tree. We'll stay here tonight."

"Oh no!" gasped the monkey king. He held his finger to his lips. Everybody would have to keep very quiet.

"You little ones must keep perfectly still – and silent," he whispered.

As the human king lay down to sleep he took one last look at the branches above. There, in the moonlight, he could clearly see ... a tail, a monkey's, hanging down.

"There are monkeys in MY tree." he shouted.

"They'll eat all my mangoes. Quickly! Light some fires. Tomorrow we can eat roast monkeys with our fruit."

The monkeys began to shake with fear.

"What are we to do?" they asked. "There's no hope for us now."

"The king and his men are going to keep watch all night," cried a little one.

"If we climb down the tree they'll catch us," sobbed another.

"Don't be afraid," whispered the monkey king, "I have a plan. Stay here."

The monkey king raced along the big branch that hung over the river. Summoning all his strength with one mighty leap he flew through the air to the other side.

Quickly, he pulled at the longest creeper. He tied one end around his waist and the other to a strong tree.

"This creeper will make a bridge for us all," he thought.

With another mighty leap, the monkey king flew back into the air.

But the creeper wasn't quite long enough and he could only just catch hold of the tip of the branch.

The monkeys watched in horror as their king hung in mid-air over the river.

"Come quickly!" he whispered." I shall be your bridge to safety."

One by one the monkeys crept along the branch and across their king's back to safety.

"Our king will surely break his back!" whispered the little monkey.

"But he won't let go," said his big sister. "Our king would rather die than lose one of us."

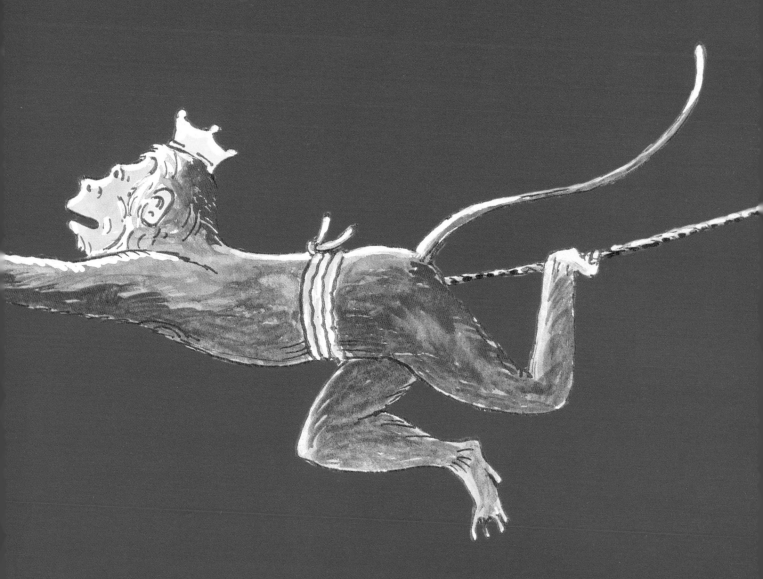

Just as the last monkey crossed over, a soldier looked up. He saw the monkey king hanging over the river. The monkey king could not move. His back was broken.
"Aha, monkey for breakfast!" laughed the soldier as he aimed his arrow.

"STOP!" called his king. "DON'T SHOOT." From his bed under the tree, he had seen everything. He had seen how the brave monkey king had risked his life to save his people.

Jumping on the raft, the human king paddled out into the river. Gently he lifted the monkey king down.

"Why did you do that?" he asked." Why did you make a bridge out of your own body?" The monkey king smiled. "My monkeys are safe now," he whispered, "That is all that matters. If you want to be a great king, you must help others."

With these words, the monkey king closed his eyes and died. As the human king sat there, holding the monkey king in his arms, his eyes filled with tears.

"This monkey has shown me how to be a real king," he said, "Let us give him a burial fit for a king."

And so it was that a great monument was built to the monkey king, so that everyone would remember his story.

notes

About the story

The story of the monkey king is one of more than 500 Jataka tales recorded in early Buddhist scriptures. It illustrates the self-sacrifice inherent in compassionate and wise leadership.

The Jataka tales are said to have been related by the Buddha to his disciples. The word Jataka (pronounced jah-ta-ka) means "relating to the birth"; these stories are traditionally said to be accounts of the past lives of the Buddha as he followed the path towards Enlightenment. Buddhists today do not necessarily see these accounts as historically true, but as pointing to deeper truths about what it means to be a human being. Most of them were probably adopted from Indian folklore because they illustrated Buddhist principles. All of them demonstrate the central Buddhist teaching of the Law of Karma: that actions have consequences. Just as selfish actions lead to suffering, kindness is its own reward.

Each of the Jataka tales begins by describing the occasion on which the story was originally told. On this particular occasion the Buddha's followers were wondering if it was true that the Buddha loved his family. Unable to agree, they went to ask him, and he responded by describing how the monkey king had heroically sacrificed his life for his family. He explained how in a past life he had been the monkey king, how the assembled followers had been his monkey family, and how he had cared for them then. In retelling the story, we have added the little monkey and his big sister as well as the initial discovery of the mango. We have left out a wicked monkey who deliberately jumps heavily on the monkey king's back while crossing over him.

Exploring the story

Adults can enhance the natural process of learning by encouraging children to talk about the story. Open-ended questions will encourage children to make an imaginative entry into the world of the story to empathize with the characters, and to make connections with their own lives.

Which part of the story did you like best, and why?

Which of the characters in the story would you most/least like to be? Why?

Why do you think ...
- the monkey king risked his life to save the others?
- the human king built a monument to the monkey king?

What do you think would have happened if ...
- the monkey king had just saved himself?
- the human king hadn't seen what the monkey king did?

Themes to develop

Putting others' needs before our own
Talk about
- what you think it means to put someone else first
- someone you know who puts other people first
- ways you can put others first

Learning from example
Talk about
- how you think the human king changed his life after the monkey king died
- what you think it means to set a good example
- whose example you follow
- how you could be a good example to others

Caring for others in the family/community
Talk about
- how people in your family/community show they care about each other
- who you care about
- how do you show you care?
- how we could care more for each other

BUDDHISM is one of the fastest-growing spiritual traditions in the Western world. Throughout its 2,500-year history, it has always succeeded in adapting its mode of expression to suit whatever culture it has encountered.

WINDHORSE PUBLICATIONS aims to continue this tradition as Buddhism comes to the West. It publishes works by authors who not only understand the Buddhist tradition but are also familiar with Western culture and the Western mind. Parents and teachers will find a wealth of background information amongst these books.

Introductory Books

Suitable introductory books include
Introducing Buddhism
by Chris Pauling

Who is the Buddha?
by Sangharakshita

What is the Dharma?
The Essential Teachings of the Buddha
by Sangharakshita

Change Your Mind
A Practical Guide to Buddhist Meditation
by Paramananda

These and many other titles are available from Windhorse Publications

Orders & catalogues

Windhorse Publications
11 Park Road,
Birmingham,
B13 8AB, UK
Tel [+44] (0)121 449 9191

Windhorse Publications Inc
540 South 2nd West,
Missoula, MT 59802, USA
Tel [+1] 406 327 0034

Windhorse Books
PO Box 574, Newtown,
NSW 2042, Australia
Tel [+61] (0)2 9519 8826

Clear Vision

The Clear Vision Trust is a Buddhist educational charity which promotes understanding of Buddhism through the visual media. Clear Vision's education team produces a range of resources, books, and videos to support high quality religious education and spiritual, moral, social, and cultural development. It also provides in-service training on Buddhism for classroom teachers. Recommended videos include the award-winning
Buddhism for Key Stage Two
and
The Monkey King and Other Tales

Clear Vision
16–20 Turner Street,
Manchester M1 4DZ, UK
Telephone
[+44] (0)161 839 9579

The FWBO

Windhorse Publications and Clear Vision are associated with the Friends of the Western Buddhist Order (FWBO). Through its sixty centres on five continents, members of the Western Buddhist Order offer meditation classes and other activities for the general public and for more experienced students. Centres also welcome school parties and teachers interested in Buddhism.
If you would like more information about the FWBO please contact
London Buddhist Centre
51 Roman Road,
London, E2 0HU, UK
Tel [+44] (0)181 981 1225

Aryaloka Retreat Center
Heartwood Circle,
Newmarket, NH 03857,
USA

In the same series

Siddhartha and the Swan

Quarrelling over a
wounded swan, the young
Prince Siddhartha helps his
cousin learn about
kindness to animals.
Beautifully illustrated, this
magical tale from the
Buddhist tradition will
entrance the younger
reader.
Illustrated by
Adiccabandhu

ISBN 1 899579 10 9
£5.99/$10.95

The Lion and the Jackal

A community of lions and
jackals learns that
friendship is built on trust
and generosity. Beautifully
illustrated, this heartening
tale from the Buddhist
tradition is retold in lively
fashion to engage the
young reader.
Illustrated by
Adiccabandhu

ISBN 1 899579 13 3
£5.99/$10.95

About the authors

Adiccabandhu is an
ordained Buddhist. An
author and illustrator, he
works for the Clear Vision
Trust, a Buddhist
educational charity. He has
over twenty years
experience in education as
teacher, trainer, and
producer of educational
resources, and has four
grown-up children of his
own.

Padmasri is an ordained
Buddhist who has enjoyed
a long career in primary
education, both as teacher
and trainer. A mother with
grown-up children of her
own, she now directs
Clear Vision's education
work.

GROWING UP

In Roman times, people often got married when they were very young. A girl might be 12 and a boy 14. A girl would offer her toys to the gods as a sign that she was no longer a child. Boys usually had a special ceremony when they were 14 to show that they were now grown up. They took off their childish clothes and *bulla* and put on adult clothes, including a toga.

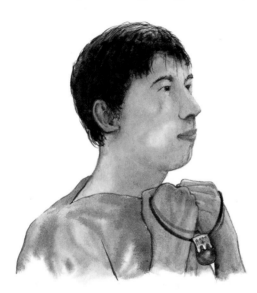

Usually a boy or girl could not choose the person they were to marry. Their parents and relatives arranged it for them. A Roman bride wore a white dress and a red veil. The bridegroom carried the bride over the threshold of their new home. This was so that the bride did not stumble—that would have been thought very unlucky.

WRITING LATIN

Latin was the language of the Romans. They spoke it in all parts of their empire. But Latin did not die out when the Roman Empire ended. It became an important language of learning. The Bible was translated into Latin, and for hundreds of years important documents were always written in Latin.

You may already know some Latin words! Many English words come from Latin, with only small changes. Languages such as Italian and Spanish are even closer to Latin than English is. You have probably used some of the letters below without knowing that they are the first letters or abbreviations of Latin words. Do you know what they mean?

PS	*post scriptum*
NB	*nota bene*
am	*ante meridiem*
pm	*post meridiem*

The answers are on page 29.

▲ Can you find any Roman names in this Latin carving?

In Roman times, important documents were written on scrolls. These were long rolls of a kind of paper, often 10 metres long. The paper was made from reeds and was called papyrus.

Papyrus was expensive, so children learning to write used writing tablets so that it didn't matter if they made a mistake. The tablets were made of wood with melted wax poured into the middle. When the wax was hard, children used a special pointed stick called a *stylus* to scratch letters on it. To use the tablet again, they used the flat end of the stick to smooth out the wax.

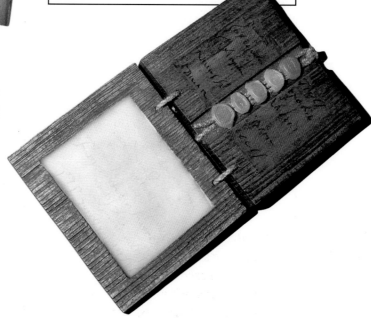

▲ This writing tablet could be closed up like a book.

MAKE A WRITING TABLET

You can use plasticine to make a writing tablet that works in the same way as a wax tablet.

You will need: a pencil and ruler ● a strong cardboard box ● a trimming knife ● glue ● some plasticine ● a rolling pin ● poster paints or felt-tip pens ● a modelling tool.

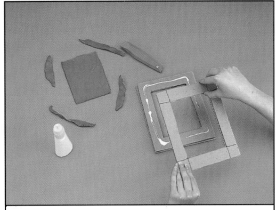

1. Draw three rectangles of the same size on the cardboard box and ask a grown-up to help cut them out carefully with the knife.

▲**2.** Put your ruler along the edge of one of the rectangles and draw a line. Do the same thing on the other sides. Cut along the lines with the knife so that you make a window. Do the same thing with *one* of the other rectangles.

3. Roll out the plasticine until it is about half a centimetre thick. Put one of the cardboard windows over the plasticine and use it as a guide to cut out a piece of plasticine the same size as the window.

▲**4.** Glue the pieces of card together as in the picture, and put the plasticine rectangle in the middle. You can put a little bit of extra plasticine round the edges to make sure it doesn't fall out.

5. Decorate the edges of your writing tablet with paints or felt tips. Use the modelling tool as a *stylus*. You can write with the pointed end and smooth out your writing again with the flat end.

DRESS LIKE A ROMAN

Roman men and women wore all sorts of different clothes. It depended on where they came from, how rich they were, and what kind of work they did.

The kinds of clothes we most often think of the Romans as wearing are those you see below. They would be worn by fairly wealthy people, probably living in a town or city.

The woman is wearing a *stola* with a *palla* over it. A *stola* was quite a simple dress, often fastened with brooches at the shoulders. The *palla* was a large shawl that could be worn in different ways. Both of them might be made of beautiful coloured materials.

The man is wearing a tunic with a *toga* over it. The *toga* was a very big half-circle of cloth that had to be carefully folded and arranged.

A STOLA AND PALLA

1. Fold one sheet in half lengthwise. Hold it up to your shoulders and ask a friend to mark where it reaches the floor. Cut across the sheet at that point.

2. Sew up the side of the sheet, but leave the top and bottom open.

You will need: two old single sheets ● scissors ● needle and thread ● string or cord ● scraps of coloured card and paper ● glue ● sticky tape ● safety pins ● a friend to help you!

▲**3.** Make some brooches by using sticky tape to fix safety pins to pieces of card cut into shapes. Decorate them with coloured paper shapes.

4. Use the brooches to pin together the top edge of your stola – but leave a space for your head!

5. Put on your stola. Tie two pieces of cord or string around you, and pull the stola up over them a bit.

6. The second sheet makes your palla. Drape it around yourself however you like, or look through this book for some ideas.

A TUNIC AND TOGA

You will need: a large T-shirt ● an old single sheet ● a felt-tip pen ● string ● scissors ● a large open space ● someone to help you!

1. Spread out the sheet on the floor. Find the middle of one of the long sides and make a small mark with a felt-tip pen. Cut a piece of string the same length as from the mark to the end of the sheet, but add a few more centimetres for making a knot.

▲2. Tie one end of the string to a felt-tip pen, and ask a friend to hold the other end at the mark on the sheet. Very slowly and carefully, stretch out the string and let the felt-tip pen mark the sheet as you move round. You will draw a half-circle. Cut along the line to make your toga.

3. Put on a large T-shirt that reaches at least to your knees. Tie a piece of string round your waist as a belt. Then ask a friend to help you put your toga on.

4. Togas were also worn in different ways, other than the pictures below. Remember, even the Romans found this difficult, so don't worry if you need to practise!

A SOLDIER'S LIFE

To conquer new lands for the empire and to keep the peace there afterwards, the Romans needed a large and skilful army. As the empire grew, the army became more and more important.

Controlling a huge number of soldiers is difficult. The Romans divided their army up into smaller groups of soldiers.

A century was a group of one hundred men, led by a centurion.

Each century was part of a cohort. Usually there were six centuries in a cohort.

Ten cohorts made up a legion. That is why soldiers were called legionaries.

In Roman times there were no trucks or aeroplanes to take soldiers to the farthest parts of the empire. They had to walk there carrying all their equipment. To make these journeys quicker and safer, the Roman army built thousands of miles of road all over the empire. These roads were so well made that some of them can still be seen today.

Most soldiers were infantry — they fought on foot. But there were also some horsemen, or cavalry, who were used for riding on ahead of the army to find the enemy.

Soldiers wore tunics and leather sandals. Over this they wore armour made of leather and metal. The armour had to be strong enough to protect them, but fairly light so that they could march long distances in it. Most soldiers carried spears and shields made of wood and leather. In colder parts of the empire, soldiers also wore woollen cloaks and leggings.

In training, soldiers practised forming different fighting groups. One of these was called a *testudo*, or "tortoise", — perhaps you can see why. It was useful if the enemy were throwing rocks or spears down from the walls of a fortress.

When they were attacking a walled city, the Romans used a huge catapult, called an *onager*, to hurl huge rocks at the walls.

Some soldiers built forts and walls as well as roads. Hadrian's Wall, which runs across the north of England, was about 73 miles long. It marked the most northerly border of the Roman Empire and made it easier to defend against Scottish tribes.

Legionaries came from all over the empire. Their lives were hard and they were often away from their families for years at a time.

There was always a danger that they would become fed up and rise up against their leaders. The emperors tried to keep them happy by paying them well and giving them a gift of money or land when they retired after 20 or 25 years of service.

FAMOUS ROMANS

JULIUS CAESAR

Born in about 100 BC, Julius Caesar was a great soldier. He helped to conquer new land for the Roman Empire, including most of what is now France. He returned to Italy in 49 BC and became the most powerful man in Rome. Some senators thought he was *too* powerful. They murdered him on 15 March 44 BC.

EMPEROR AUGUSTUS

Augustus' real name was Octavian. He was the adopted son of Julius Caesar. After Caesar's death, Octavian took power with two other men. One of these was Mark Antony. Later, these two fell out and Antony was defeated in battle. Octavian ruled alone and was given a special title: Augustus. Augustus was a clever and fair ruler who took account of the people's needs, but kept a tight control on everything. He was such a good emperor that when he died in AD14, the people did not want to go back to a republic.

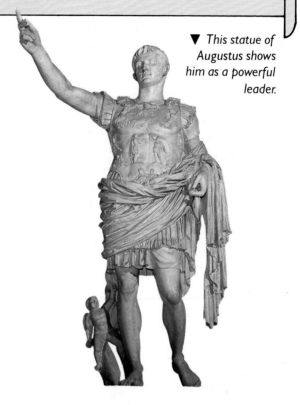

▼ *This statue of Augustus shows him as a powerful leader.*

▶ *This head of Claudius was found in a river in Suffolk, England.*

EMPEROR CLAUDIUS

Because he was often ill when he was young, Claudius led a quiet life, studying and writing history, until he was 51. Then he was made emperor because he was the only member of his family left. Although he was in some ways a strange choice, he ruled wisely until his death in AD 54. During his reign, Britain became part of the empire.

EMPEROR CONSTANTINE

After AD 305, the Roman Empire was split into an eastern empire and a western empire. Constantine the Great, as he was known, managed to unite the empire again for a while. He was the first emperor to become a Christian. He moved the capital of the empire from Rome to a new city in what is now Turkey. He called it Constantinople. Today we know it as Istanbul.

MAKE A ROMAN STATUE

Powerful Romans had statues of themselves set up in public places so that people would remember them. In Roman times, these statues were often painted in gold and bright colours, but the colours have since faded and today we only see the colour of the stone.

You will need: a one-metre piece of plastic-covered wire ● some plasticine ● wallpaper paste ● cotton wool ● cotton material ● pencil ● scissors ● wool or string ● poster paint.

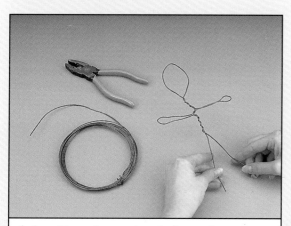

▲ **1.** To make a wire skeleton for your statue, first fold the piece of wire in half. Then bend and twist the wire to make a figure like the one in the picture.

2. Mix the wallpaper paste with water to make a fairly stiff paste. Tear or cut some of your material into strips, dip them in the glue, and then wind them round your wire skeleton. You can put some cotton wool round the wire to make the head and stomach fatter.

3. Before the paste dries, bend the statue's arms and head into the right positions for your statue.

4. Cut a strip of material as long as your statue, but not too wide. Make a hole in the middle, dip it in the paste, and slip it over the statue's head. Overlap the sides and tie a piece of wool or string round your statue's waist.

5. Now spread out the rest of your material and draw a half-circle on it. The straight edge should be about three times as long as your statue. This is the statue's toga. Cut out the half-circle and dip it in the paste. Then drape the toga around your statue. Look at page 22 to see how to do this.

6. Make a mound of plasticine and push the legs of your statue into it. Leave it somewhere warm to dry until the paste has set hard. Then paint your statue.

27

THE END OF THE EMPIRE

Keeping order in the huge Roman Empire was always difficult. Many conquered people were unhappy under Roman rule and tried to rebel. The Roman army was kept busy acting as a police force throughout the empire. But problems came from *outside* the empire too. The Romans called people from beyond the empire barbarians. The barbarians were always attacking the borders of the empire, especially from the north.

By AD 300, the Romans had divided the empire in an attempt to control it better. One emperor ruled the western empire from Rome, while another emperor ruled the eastern empire from Constantinople. But all the time barbarians were attacking the borders and invading further and further into the empire. The Romans could not defend themselves on all sides at once.

In AD 455, Rome itself was seized by the barbarians, and just over 20 years later a German leader took over from the last western emperor. Strangely, this last emperor's name was a reminder of the very first days of Rome. It was Romulus Augustulus.

The eastern empire lasted much longer. It became known as the Byzantine Empire and kept many Roman customs and the Christian religion. But the eastern empire ended too, in 1453, when it was conquered by the Turks and became Muslim.

DID YOU KNOW?

SCRAPING, NOT SOAPING!

The Romans did not have soap. Instead, they covered their bodies with oil and then scraped the oil off with a special tool called a *strigil*. Dirt and dead skin came off with the oil. Rich people had a slave to do the scraping for them!

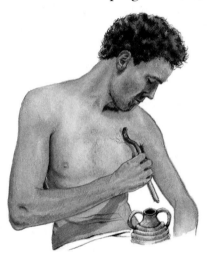

LATIN WORDS

post scriptum means "after writing" — a PS is something you add after you have finished writing a letter.

nota bene means "note well" — NB is used to point out something important.

ante meridiem (am) means "before noon" — morning in other words! You can guess what *post meridiem* (pm) means.

ROMAN NUMBERS

Although the Romans were brilliant engineers, they were less good at maths! This was because they used a system of numbers that were very awkward to do sums with. You can still sometimes see Roman numerals on clocks or sundials.

THE ROMAN CALENDAR

Our calendar is based on the Roman one. Like us, they had 365 days in a year, a leap year every four years, and twelve months. Here are the names of the Roman months. Do they look familiar?

Januarius
Februarius
Martialis
Aprilis
Maius
Junius
Julius
Augustus
September
October
November
December

1	I
2	II
3	III
4	IV
5	V
6	VI
7	VII
8	VIII
9	IX
10	X
11	XI
12	XII

Can you see which two months were named after famous Roman leaders? Page 26 will give you a clue.

GLOSSARY

Abbreviation — A short way of saying or writing a word.

Amphitheatre — A building in which shows were put on. It was usually built in a circle. Rows of seats rising around the space for the shows in the middle meant that everybody could see.

Amphorae — Pointed pottery jars for holding wine or oil.

Archaeologist — Someone who finds out about the past by looking at the buildings and objects that people have left behind.

Atrium — The hallway of a house, often open to the sky.

Barbarian — The Roman name for anyone who did not live in the Roman Empire.

Bulla — A lucky charm hung around the neck of a baby.

Cavalry — Soldiers who fought on horseback.

Centurion — Leader of a century.

Century — A group of 100 soldiers in the Roman army, led by a centurion.

Chariot — A cart with two wheels, pulled by horses.

Cohort — A group of about 600 soldiers in the Roman army.

Consul — A ruler in the time of the Roman republic. There were usually two consuls, who were in charge of the army and the laws.

Democracy — A country in which the people vote to decide who should be their leaders.

Emperor — The ruler of the Roman Empire.

Forum — The main square of a Roman town, where business was done.

Gladiator — A man (usually a slave) who was made to fight in a show to entertain people.

Infantry — Soldiers who fought on foot.

Legion — A group of nearly 6,000 soldiers, or legionaries, in the Roman army. A legion was made up of six cohorts.

Mosaic — A picture or pattern made of many small pieces of stone set in plaster.

Palla — A large shawl worn by Roman women.

Papyrus — A kind of paper made from reeds pressed together.

Pestle and mortar — A mortar is a strong bowl in which spices and other food can be crushed into a powder. The pestle is like a very heavy stick that pounds the food.

Republic — A country where the people choose their own leaders.

Senator — A member of the senate, which was the body of men who gave advice to the consuls during the Roman republic.

Slave — A person who had no rights in Roman times. Slaves were owned by their masters but were sometimes given their freedom.

Stola — A long dress worn by Roman women.

Stylus — A pointed stick for writing on a wax tablet.

RESOURCES

PLACES TO VISIT
There are traces of the Romans in many parts of Britain. Ask your library or tourist information centre if there is anywhere close by that you can visit. Many museums hold collections of Roman objects, of which a few are listed below.

British Museum
Great Russell Street
London
WC1B 3DG
Visit this vast museum which has many rooms dedicated to Roman objects.

Corinium Museum
Park Street
Cirencester
GL7 2BX
Cirencester, called 'Corinium' by the Romans, was the second largest town in Roman Britain. Visit the museum to experience life as a Roman.

Roman Baths
Pump Room
Stall Street
Bath
BA1 1LZ
Visit the Roman baths and museum to find out about this Roman religious spa.

Vindolanda and the Roman Army Museum
Greenhead
Carlisle
Haltwhistle
CA8 7JB
Situated along Hadrian's Wall, Vindolanda is the site of a Roman fort and settlement. Learn about life as a Roman soldier in the Roman Army Museum.

USEFUL WEBSITES
www.bbc.co.uk/schools/romans
This BBC site includes information, activities and games about the Romans.

www.historyonthenet.com/Romans/romansmain.htm
This site is packed with information about the Romans in Britain.

www.thebritishmuseum.ac.uk/explore/online_tours.aspx
Click on 'Rome' and then choose from chariot-racing or gladiators.

Note to parents and teachers: Every effort has been made by the Publishers to ensure that these websites are suitable for children, that they are of the highest educational value, and that they contain no inappropriate or offensive material. However, because of the nature of the Internet, it is impossible to guarantee that the contents of these sites will not be altered. We strongly advise that Internet access is supervised by a responsible adult.

INDEX

amphitheatre 6, 30
amphorae 11, 30
aqueduct 7
armour 24
army 24, 25, 28
art 12
atrium 8, 30

barbarians 28, 30
bath-house 6
bulla 18, 19, 30

calendar 29
cavalry 24, 30
centurion 24, 30
chariot racing 14, 30
Christianity 7, 28
clothes 22
cohort 24, 30
consuls 5, 30

democracy 5, 30
drink 10, 11

Emperor Augustus 5, 26
        Claudius 26
        Constantine the Great 12, 26

food 10, 11
forum 7, 30

gladiator fights 14, 30

homes 7

infantry 24, 30

Jesus 4
Julius Caesar 26

Latin 20, 29
legion 24, 30
legionaries 24, 25

Mark Antony 26
marriage 19
masks 16, 17
mosaics 12, 13, 14, 30

numerals 29

Octavian 26
onager 25

palla 22, 23, 30
papyrus 20, 30
pestle and mortar 10, 30

Remus 5
River Tiber 5
roads 4, 24
Rome 5
Romulus 5

school 18
scrolls 20
senator 5, 26, 30
slaves 5, 10, 30
sport 14
statues 12, 27
stola 22, 23, 30
strigil 29
stylus 20, 21, 30

theatre 16
thermae 6
toga 19, 22, 23
towns 4, 6, 7, 12
toys 18
tunic 22, 23

villa 8, 9

writing tablet 20, 21

Additional photographs: The Ancient Art and Architecture Collection 12(b), 20(both);
C.M. Dixon 5, 12(t), 14(b), 26(both); Michael Holford 14(t), 16; Zefa 28.